The Money Game:
Financing Collegiate Athletics

The Money Game:
Financing Collegiate Athletics

**By Robert H. Atwell,
Bruce Grimes,
and Donna A. Lopiano**

60778

AMERICAN COUNCIL ON EDUCATION
WASHINGTON, D. C.

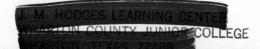

© 1980 by the American Council on Education
One Dupont Circle, Washington, D. C. 20036

Library of Congress Cataloging in Publication Data
Atwell, Robert H
    The money game.

    1. College sports—United States—Finance.
I. Grimes, Bruce, joint author.   II. Lopiano,
Donna A., joint author.   III. Title.
GV350.A88   796   80-15484
ISBN 0-8268-1445-X

9 8 7 6 5 4 3 2 1

Printed in the United States of America

Contents

Foreword

All of us in the higher education community are keenly aware of the publicity and interest focused on campus athletics programs. In particular, the role money plays in collegiate athletics has received great attention in the media.

The American Council on Education's Commission on Collegiate Athletics felt that the increasing emphasis on money and the problems it presents warranted greater analysis. At the request of the Commission, this study was undertaken by three persons—Robert H. Atwell, vice president of the American Council on Education; Bruce Grimes, director of athletics at the University of Wisconsin, Green Bay; and Donna A. Lopiano, director of intercollegiate athletics for women at the University of Texas, Austin. Its purpose was to examine how and why money is spent and to illuminate the financial future of collegiate athletics. I hope it will provide insights into the athletics situation. It is not an official pronouncement of the Council, but rather an attempt to bring together information, observations, and some opinions from persons interested in the health and welfare of collegiate athletics and the colleges and universities that sponsor the programs.

The study was made possible through a generous grant from the Carnegie Corporation of New York. The American Council on Education and the authors are grateful for the time and information supplied by the athletics directors and other administrators at the universities they visited. Particular thanks is extended to E. Alden Dunham of the Carnegie Corporation for his continuing interest and support. The authors acknowledge with gratitude the important contribution of Laura A. Wilson to this study.

J. W. PELTASON, *President*
American Council on Education

Introduction

Nationally, intercollegiate athletics is a small part of the higher education budget. Too, the number of participants in intercollegiate athletics is a small portion of the total student enrollment nationwide—probably less than 5 percent. Expenditures for intercollegiate athletics amount to $500 million, or less than 1 percent of the total expenditures for all colleges and universities.

But because of the attention lavished on the athletics programs of perhaps one-twentieth of all higher education institutions in the country—and that attention is largely focused on the football or basketball programs of these institutions—intercollegiate athletics has assumed far more importance than the participation rates or dollars expended would seem to justify. This importance has been a function of television and subsequent changing of sports into entertainment. In 1978, over 34 million spectators attended football games between four-year institutions belonging to the National Collegiate Athletics Association (NCAA). The television sets of an average of nearly 9 million homes are tuned to ABC's Saturday television game, which is about 35 percent of the market during that prime time. Television has also helped transform intercollegiate athletics at relatively few institutions into big business. The ABC contract with the NCAA to televise football games currently produces $30 million annually for the participating athletics programs. A similar contract for the NCAA Division I basketball playoffs will reportedly produce an added $18 million for those institutions.

Thus, a large share of the public receives an impression of a few colleges and universities only through watching intercollegiate football or basketball games. This impression is reinforced by limited coverage in newspapers and on local and national television. The pressure is considerable on college and university chief executive officers in these institutions to produce *winning* teams. Winning not only enhances good public relations with alumni and other supporters, but is also often necessary to produce the gate receipts that account for more than half of the income needed to support the athletics programs of the 180 institutions that participate in NCAA Division I football. Only a handful of institutions have consistently attracted large attendance for losing teams. A winning team is a necessity for success at the gate. Football stadia seat far more people than basketball arenas; therefore, the overwhelming share of gate receipt income (about 85 percent in NCAA Division I football institutions) comes from football. Although football is by far the most expensive intercollegiate sport, for most of the major institutions it is the only sport capable of generating substantially more income than is required to conduct the sport. Basketball is a budgetary winner for some institutions but net income from basketball is rarely sufficiently large to carry a significant portion of the costs of nonrevenue-producing sports. In perhaps eighty to ninety institutions, football must support the entire intercollegiate athletics program for men and women. Only a handful of these institutions more than break even in their total multisport athletics program and yet all of them are struggling to increase gate receipts.

The percentage of male student athletes participating in NCAA Division I sports is about one-sixth of all male student athletes. Male athletes in the high-pressure sports of football and basketball at about 260 institutions with NCAA Division I programs account for less than 10 percent of the total male participants in all intercollegiate sports. However, the large institutions in which these small numbers of highly talented athletes perform account for about 22 percent of the total enrollment in nonprofit postsecondary institutions. The events in which these few athletes perform account for as much as 75 percent of the attendance at intercollegiate athletic events. The sixty-two institutions belonging to the College Football Association (CFA), an organization of most major football powers, account for 10 percent of the enrollment in colleges and universities.

Even though the growth in numbers of sports for women and their participation have increased in the last few years at rates in excess of those for men, only about 100,000 women are involved in intercollegiate sports—nearly a three-to-one participation ratio in favor of men. Moreover, women's programs are not very visible because few people attend women's events—though attendance appears to be improving—and thus women's programs do not generate much income. In fact, in the NCAA Division I institutions, the typical women's program depends somewhat on the financial success of men's football for budgetary support, although most of the funds for women's programs come from institutional sources rather than gate receipts.

It is clear that a few football and basketball programs in a few institutions, involving a small proportion of the total number of student athletes, take up disproportionate public attention as manifested in the sports pages, on television, and in attendance at events. For most student athletes in most programs in most institutions, intercollegiate athletics is simply another activity in their lives. They are students first and they receive no financial aid based on their prowess as athletes. The programs in which they participate do not generate significant gate receipts and are funded from the same sources—tuition, state appropriations, unrestricted gifts, and investment income—that support the institution as a whole. With the exception of the potential impact of complying with Title IX of the Education Amendments of 1972, forbidding sex discrimination in institutions which receive federal funds, the financial problems of intercollegiate athletics programs of most colleges and universities are part of the general financial problems of the institutions. Athletics in most institutions are not intended to be self-supporting and most events involve few, if any, spectators.

Those few institutions, however, with highly visible and intensive athletics programs have some unique financial problems that may be distinguishable from an institution's other financial problems. This possibility is one motive for this report. We considered whether the athletics programs had different financial problems than the rest of the institution. At least the multiplicity of funding sources and the necessity of generating gate receipts or restricted gifts may create more difficulties for athletics programs than is true of other programs in these institutions.

Interinstitutional comparisons of financial data are always hazardous in higher education because of the autonomy of individual institutions and the diversity of institutional types. In recent years, the Higher Education General Information Survey (HEGIS) conducted by the National Center for Education Statistics (NCES) of the U.S. Department of Health, Education, and Welfare has brought some standardization to financial reporting, although the quality of much of the reporting is somewhat suspect. The American Institute of Certified Public Accountants (AICPA) has published an audit guide for colleges and universities, the issuance of which has also done much to standardize the financial reporting.

None of these national efforts has influenced the comparability of financial reporting in athletics. Several factors may help explain why interinstitutional comparisons are more difficult in athletics than in most other areas of college and university finance. Most athletics departments apparently do not have access to the kind of analytic capacity that can produce data useful for comparisons.

Many of the departments—athletics or academic—that have such a capacity have not been eager to share information. In a few cases, such secrecy might be a function of success; the athletics program has made a profit, which the administrator wants to hide from the faculty and some other interests within the institution. Or the managers of unprofitable athletics programs might want to obscure their dependence on general fund subventions or restricted gifts. Intercollegiate athletics is an area of university operations that tends to be shrouded in secrecy.

Perhaps the most decisive factor that prohibits financial comparisons in athletics is the multiplicity of funding sources in the big-time programs and the lack of any consensus on how to report costs by program.

Data sources

That each institution keeps its own books in accordance with its own needs and, in the case of state institutions and community colleges, in accordance with external requirements, has not encouraged the development of reporting systems to permit sport-by-sport expenditure and income projections in light of standard definitions and universal systems for allocating overhead costs. Some conferences, most notably the Western Athletic Conference, have cooperated in the exchange of certain program indicators including, but not limited to, financial information. The only credible national study of which we are aware is by Mitchell Raiborn. His work was supported and published by the NCAA.[1] The more recent study, *Revenues and Expenses of Intercollegiate Athletic Programs*, covers the years 1970–77 and is based on questionnaires completed by 330 of NCAA's 722 members as of September 1977.[2] We are most grateful for the Raiborn studies, which provide useful information, although they have by no means overcome the problems of comparisons in this field. We concluded at the outset of our study that, while we would ask the

1. Mitchell H. Raiborn, *Financial Aspects of Intercollegiate Athletics* (Shawnee Mission, Kans.: National Collegiate Athletic Association, 1970).
2. Raiborn, *Revenues and Expenses of Intercollegiate Athletic Programs: Analysis of Trends and Relationships 1970–1977* (Shawnee Mission, Kans.: National Collegiate Athletic Association, 1978).

same questions at each institution we visited, we would not expect to obtain, nor did we, the kind of financial data that would permit program-by-program comparisons. Although we collected massive amounts of information, we have no consistent data base of the sort that would permit unit cost comparison.

Athletics governance

Throughout the study, reference is made to the national governing organizations in intercollegiate athletics. The best known organization is the National Collegiate Athletic Association (NCAA) founded in 1906 with about 733 active institutional members. The newest and now the largest governing body in athletics is the Association for Intercollegiate Athletics for Women (AIAW), founded in 1971, which has over 970 members. The National Association of Intercollegiate Athletics (NAIA), founded in 1940, now has 520 members, mostly the smaller colleges. The National Junior College Athletic Association has nearly 600 members; the 104 community colleges in California have a separate governing structure. Most NCAA members also belong to AIAW and there is about 20 percent overlap between NCAA and NAIA membership. Thus, about half of the nation's roughly 3,000 accredited two- and four-year nonprofit colleges and universities belong to one of these national governing structures. However, these member institutions represent far more than half of the 11 million students enrolled in all colleges and universities in America.

Organization of the report

The report is organized in three major parts. In the first part, an athletics typology is presented that comprises six types of institutions: semi-professional; Ivy League; small college; mixed; predominantly black; and community college. In the second part, we discuss some of the major income sources for athletics, particularly gate receipts, television fees, and gifts. Then, in part three, some of the major expenditure variables are reviewed, including travel and grants-in-aid to athletes. We have also included a section on women's athletics in this part. The report closes with our conclusions and recommendations.

Method

For reasons set forth earlier on the lack of comparability of financial data, we concluded that the basic method we would use in the study would be to visit a range of colleges and universities with athletics programs which were reasonably representative of intercollegiate athletics typology. Timing and scheduling did not permit each of us to visit each institution of the thirty selected, and Ms. Lopiano and Mr. Atwell wish to acknowledge that Mr. Grimes visited more institutions than they were able to visit. During the course of these visits, a standardized set of questions was asked of athletics directors and chief executive officers or their representatives. These visits, together with our own experiences as athletics or academic administrators, are the basis of the conclusions we are presenting. Except where otherwise indicated, we all share the major conclusions of the report.

We have not addressed the abuses of rules that can crop up in intercollegiate sports—indeed, all sports—because of pressures to produce winners. Readers are aware of investigations of illegalities involving intercollegiate sports at several schools. We do not touch on the issues raised by those proceedings. Our task has been to comment on the larger financial future of intercollegiate athletics in light of economic trends and equal opportunity legislation.

The views expressed are solely our responsibility and are not necessarily shared by the Commission on Collegiate Athletics, the American Council on Education, the universities at which Mr. Grimes and Ms. Lopiano hold appointments, or the Carnegie Corporation of New York.

Finally, we want to express our respect for the governing associations in intercollegiate athletics. At various points in this report, we offer some comments that are critical of certain of their policies and practices. We wish to make clear that these associations have made invaluable contributions in promoting athletics and in reconciling the inevitably competing values and objectives that characterize much of intercollegiate athletics.

An Athletics Typology

The athletics programs in the nation's colleges and universities are diverse. They vary by size, purpose, accouterment, quality, and so on. Yet, it is possible to classify the programs into six types that roughly correspond to the various divisions and conferences established by the intercollegiate athletics governing bodies:

Semiprofessional—Perhaps 260 institutions belong in this category. They hold membership in the NCAA Division I and are distinguished by highly competitive football and basketball programs that are expected to produce substantial gate receipts.

Ivy League—Only eight universities belong to the Ivy League. The principal distinguishing characteristic of these schools is that they do not award athletics grants-in-aid as the semipro and mixed schools do, but still maintain a competitiveness that is at a higher level than most of the remaining kinds of institutions.

Small college—About 700 four-year, mostly private institutions are included under this designation. The athletics programs are participatory in character, generate little or no income, and are closely tied to the academic program.

Mixed—At least 250 institutions fall into this classification. Their athletics programs have some of the characteristics of the semipro programs and have similarities with other models.

Predominantly black—Almost all of the 115 to 120 predominantly black colleges and universities offer athletics programs of varying types that correspond to the other models described here. Because of the history and unique financial problems of black higher education in America, the status and functioning of these programs are treated separately here.

Community college—About 700 two-year institutions participate in intercollegiate athletics. That they are two-year colleges with their own athletics governing body is the chief characteristic that distinguishes them from other institutions.

The Semiprofessional Intercollegiate Athletics Model

No slur is intended by the use of the words *semipro* or *semiprofessional* to describe those intercollegiate athletics programs that have become important assets for the mostly public universities that support them from both a financial and a public relations perspective.[3] It is essential to both acknowledge and define these semipro programs as being very different from traditional intercollegiate athletics, which focus on competitive sports as student-centered activities within a relatively pure educational environment. The semipro programs are money machines: for most of this century, educators have been considerably concerned about the commercial and entertainment value of these programs. At the same time, semipro collegiate athletics have been invaluable public relations and fund-raising tools of institutions that have become increasingly concerned about maximizing their income.

This positive view of the semipro programs has seldom been emphasized. Instead, commercialized athletics programs have received unbridled criticism from within and outside the academic community. Regularly over the last fifty years, the public and educators alike have called for a stop to "this commercial madness," and a return to the "good old days" when athletics was mainly a diversion for the serious student. Solving the financial and philosophical problems of semipro intercollegiate athletics programs rests upon the ability of members of the higher education community to understand the commercial aspect and positive function of these programs as they relate to institutional goals and to retain their positive contributions while also discovering how to control their manifest and latent abuses. Few athletics programs are totally commercial. Only one or two revenue-producing and spectator-oriented

3. Neither do we mean to imply that student athletes are paid at the semipro institutions (although some people might argue that the grants-in-aid awarded are pay). Rather, we use the term narrowly—that is, to reflect the expectation in these schools that some of the athletics programs—principally football and/or basketball—are to make money to cover their costs.

men's "major" sports within such programs deserve the semipro label, an important fact to keep in mind. (Women's athletics programs have not yet entered the semipro arena.)

Semipro men's athletics programs seem to be committed to being nationally competitive at the highest level in one or more sports (usually football and basketball) and to spending maximum permissible funds under governing body rules. The average total budget for NCAA Division I football programs was approximately $2.2 million in 1977 and $317,000 in Division I institutions with major basketball programs but no football programs.[4] Only 263 of the over 720 NCAA institutions are classified as Division I (178 have Division I football and 85 do not). Football programs are further classified as Division IA or IAA. Of the 139 athletics programs with Division IA football, 80 are significantly "richer" than Division IAA football programs in that their revenues and expenditures are almost double that of the average Division I program.

Division I programs are, therefore, difficult to characterize financially because of the effect of football. Common to these programs is the concept of "major" and "minor" sports. "Major" sports such as football and basketball and, in some cases, ice hockey, wrestling, and soccer, are provided almost unlimited resources because they have been traditionally successful over a long period and continue to draw enthusiastic spectator interest.

Many public institutions with semipro programs that have opted for Division IA football finance five, six, or more nationally competitive sports in addition to the same or greater number of minor sports. The typical budgets of such programs range from $3.5 to $8 million—considerably higher than the average budget of all programs in the category. These programs are more likely to be in the "black." This wealthy sector must be kept in perspective as data for and characteristics of the semipro model are discussed. For this group, any average figures are deceptively low.

In 1977, according to Mitchell Raiborn's NCAA study, about 58 percent of the programs with football and 25 percent of the programs without football were making money, with average profit margins of $281,000 and $138,000 respectively.[5] However, this rosy financial picture is darkened by deficits of programs not making money: the average deficits were $553,000 (with football) and $226,000 (without football)—almost double

4. Raiborn, *Revenues and Expenses of Intercollegiate Athletic Programs.*
5. *Ibid.,* p. 9 and p. 14.

the profits for the financially healthy programs. Herein lies the problem with the semipro model: the rich are getting richer and the poor are getting poorer. More importantly, Raiborn predicts this trend will continue with corresponding increases in profits and deficits at least over the next five years. Long-term financial data are not available for women's athletics programs. Raiborn's report barely mentions the subject and recent data published by the Association for Intercollegiate Athletics for Women only scratch the surface.[6]

The average semipro institution has a women's athletics program involving 130 athletes and eight sports and a budget in 1977 of $276,000 (including salaries, wages, and scholarships). This budget represents about 14 percent of the total athletics budget—up from 2 percent in 1973–74. Female athletes make up 30 percent of the athletic population. Program data are so sparse as to preclude accurate growth projections for the next several years.

This basic financial picture is essential to understanding the semipro athletics program model. These multimillion dollar investments do not have as their primary purpose providing athletic opportunities for student athletes. Rather, without exception, representatives of the institutions visited made it clear that athletics was considered an extremely valuable institutional asset that is marketed and sold to the public for dollars and influence. A secondary dimension, then, is the provision of highly sophisticated sports training opportunities for students.

Semipro programs are usually structured as self-supporting auxiliary enterprises that have no formal attachment to the traditional academic structure of the university. A few institutions have tied their programs to physical education departments. It is not unusual for most programs to use split appointments between athletics and physical education for minor sports coaches. The athletics director is programmatically responsible to a faculty athletics council, which may also include alumni and student representatives. The program is directly under a university vice president or the president. University trustees or boards of regents are also closely involved with the athletics program, although such interest and influence is seldom depicted on the organizational charts of these universities.

Revenue-producing sports programs typically spend and bring in at least half of the athletics operating budget. Annual debt service expend-

6. Association for Intercollegiate Athletics for Women, *Competitive Division Structure Implementation Survey* (Washington: The Association, 1978), p. 11.

itures for capital improvements make up 10–12 percent of the total budget. Operating expense budgets usually do not include such expenditures. The single largest category of operating expense is salaries and wages (25–30 percent), followed closely by athletics scholarships (18–20 percent), and recruiting/travel (12–15 percent).

Gate receipts represent 50 percent of all income while guarantees, television, and bowl receipts account for an additional 10–15 percent. Student fees account for only 10 percent of program income at institutions with football programs, but 20 percent at institutions without football. Alumni contributions are growing and account for 5–10 percent of the total income. Unlike other athletics program models, little, if any, institutional or government support is funneled into operating budgets. If institutional monies are used, these are usually restricted to salaries and/or scholarships. The predominant financial policy is to be self-supporting.

It is important to note that the institution's support of the athletics program usually takes the form of providing physical plant and utilities. Several athletics programs actually charge some physical plant costs to the university, and several are even totally separate corporate enterprises, funding all of their building and operating costs. Less than half of the institutions with such programs are private universities, which spend considerably more on scholarships than their public university counterparts due to higher tuition costs. Public institutions have smaller scholarship budgets because of state government-subsidized tuitions and, in several cases, tuition waiver programs for out-of-state student athletes. One of the realities of big-time intercollegiate athletics is that, except for such universities as the University of Southern California and Notre Dame, private institutions have been chased out of the market by high costs, particularly their much higher tuition costs, which must be paid on behalf of athletes given grants-in-aids.

In the past decade, gate receipts have declined in the percentage of total budget but have been offset by increased contributions from alumni and other supporters. Without exception, all institutions visited were seeking to increase these gift income sources as opposed to decreasing expenses. They recognize that the effect of inflation and the projected cost of providing equal opportunity for women will require significant additional resources. Greater than normal inflationary increases in scholarship and salary areas and the cost of Title IX compliance were pointed to as the most critical financial concerns.

Common to the profit-making or self-supporting programs is the existence of significant reserves that were established to insure against the "bad season," which might result in decreased gate receipt income. At many institutions, these reserves have been severely depleted in the past few years. The contribution of the semipro athletics model to the academic institution is considerable. It is important to understand why and how semipro athletics developed into an institutional asset and how its current status has resulted in loss of institutional autonomy in the control of program expenditures and practices.

Institutions have had to give up a large degree of control of intercollegiate athletics programs to the NCAA and other athletics governing bodies because of the interinstitutional nature of these programs and the need for consistent rules governing their operations. The NCAA successfully promoted and marketed collegiate sports and significantly increased gate receipt and television income to the semipro athletics programs of member institutions. A degree of program control was sold to the visual media for a considerable sum. The media, in turn, educated the public and sold sports to supporters who, wishing to be identified with "a winner," contributed additional resources to individual institutions. To obtain large or annual contributions, institutions sold all sorts of perquisites (tickets, priority seating, parking, and other privileges) and influence to obtain additional alumni resources. These practices resulted in the loss of more control over the program. If alumni were not satisfied with a football win/loss record and wanted action to remove the head football coach, they succeeded because they threatened to withhold necessary resources. In addition, television was a good image tool for universities, particularly as it affected legislative funding.

It was only a matter of time before the pressures of both the media and the public interest became too intense for individual institutions to handle. Any unilateral effort to control costs was doomed to failure because it would put institutions at a competitive disadvantage with other institutions and start a "losers" chain reaction of less television income, less alumni interest, fewer gate receipts, less legislative influence, and a negative influence on the "quality/excellence" reputation of the university. In addition to the impossibility of individual institutions unilaterally cutting costs, the financial stability of intercollegiate semipro athletics programs could be significantly undermined by *one* institution increasing its expenditures in order to recruit student athletes or make its facilities, program, or schedule more attractive to student athletes. Other institutions had to follow suit to maintain competitiveness. The "keep up with the Jones" syndrome began and added even more pressure by forcing institutions to seek the necessary financial resources to keep up with practices of other institutions.

If individual institutions do not really control intercollegiate athletics, who does? The answers are: (1) the athletics governing bodies that were given control of athletics by these institutions, and (2) alumni and spectators who provide resources. These forces constitute the financial dilemma and crisis facing semipro programs. The athletics governing bodies have not acted in any significant ways to control costs because the "haves" in the system do not want to risk losing their competitive advantage to the "have-nots." Unless proposed cost-cutting actions affect all institutions equally (to date no cost-control proposals have included such guarantees), thereby maintaining the existing competition picture, those actions simply will not be passed by state legislatures. As a result, institutions have become increasingly dependent on commercial behavior to maintain their current expenditure levels: more promotions, more effective marketing strategies, more and more shares of the institutional assets sold to donors, television, and the holders of needed resources to fund uncontrolled growth. Plug in the factors of inflation and the provision of equal opportunity for women, also on a semipro expenditure level, and a prediction of financial disaster in the near future would be easily understood.

The solution to the impending financial dilemma is not the elimination of the semipro model but, rather, controlling it so that it continues to benefit institutions without driving them to bankruptcy. The only hope for such a solution is that athletics governing bodies act at the earliest moment to control semipro athletics. However, precedent does not suggest that such control is likely to occur.

The root of the problem of dependence on gate receipts and external funding sources stems from the refusal of higher education institutions with semipro programs to regard sports as a valid component of the educational programs that should be structured and financed in a manner similar to academic departments. The consequences of such a move would be to align coaching and faculty salaries, mandate standard institutional accounting procedures, and apply the same checks and balances to athletics that control the growth of any academic area. The chances of faculties and institutions revising the mind/body dichotomy that has dominated educational philosophy is probably negligible given the present financial plight of most universities. Therefore, any chance of regaining a total educational perspective of intercollegiate sports and of being able to rid athletics of its commercial manifestations is miniscule.

The Ivy League

The eight Ivy League schools are a special case not only because of their prestige, but also because they present some interesting problems that go beyond the few institutions involved. Ivy League schools are distinguishable from other major universities that participate in NCAA Division IA (football) chiefly by their not awarding any financial aid solely on the basis of athletic prowess. Recruiting is very intense; in some sports at some institutions, the pressure to win compares with that of high-intensity programs in major athletics powers that award grants-in-aid to athletes.

Ivy League schools are able to recruit despite the lack of financial aid partly because of their prestige and partly because the financially poorest students will receive a lot of financial aid on a needs basis. Sometimes, a student's decision to go Ivy League can depend on whether a student athlete believes that the prestige may be worth the self-help (loan and work) portion of a financial aid package that is granted "free" in other institutions. Student athletes must be able to survive academically in very competitive institutions, in which there may be no opportunity to major in easy subjects.

The lack of grants-in-aid for Ivy League athletes may be the principal factor in explaining why Ivy League football is not up to the quality of play in other major conferences. Another reason for the difference in play between Ivy League and other schools is that League schools have problems attracting minority athletes to what they perceive to be the alien atmosphere of an overwhelming white Princeton, New Jersey or Hanover, New Hampshire. The University of Pennsylvania can attract black basketball players from the Philadelphia area while Dartmouth cannot.

The Ivy League is characterized by large numbers of sports (Dartmouth has fifteen sports for men and thirteen for women) and very high participation rates. (Dartmouth has 950 men and 320 women participating in athletics.) An Ivy League university will spend as much as $2.5 million on its intercollegiate athletics program, which is comparable to that of other major athletics powers except for the grants-in-aid costs comparable institutions incur. A typical Ivy League institution may not produce any more than $500,000 to $700,000 in income of which not more than half may come from football. Football attendance at Ivy League institutions has fallen off somewhat recently through some combination of the declining quality of their programs compared with the quality of play at institutions with semipro programs and competition with the professionals and other entertainment alternatives in the major urban areas of New York, New Haven, Boston, and Philadelphia. Even without having to cover grants-in-aid costs, football is generally not a break-even sport in the Ivy League, nor is any other sport except for a few, such as basketball at the University of Pennsylvania or hockey at Dartmouth. In some cases, the athletics budget supports activities that may include but go well beyond intercollegiate programs, such as sailing at Brown or an expensive skiing program at Dartmouth.

In the Ivy League, as in the liberal arts colleges, athletics is not expected to be self-supporting and typically is subject to the same budgetary review and constraints as other programs of the institution. An Ivy League institution will spend $1.5 million to $2 million of unrestricted income (tuition, gifts, and investment income) on athletics. This expenditure may or may not include the costs of maintaining physical facilities since many of the facilities are multipurpose and there is no need to engage in sophisticated cost accounting when the same source of funds pays most of the costs regardless of the kind of use.

Ivy League athletics directors face some irreconcilable pressures. They are expected to produce sufficient income to hold down further drains on the institutional budgets in universities that deemphasize sports. Such competing demands make it difficult to produce winners on the field or at the gate. They are expected to offer a larger number of sports than is financially possible at a time when ticket sales are not rising as rapidly as costs. Despite a potentially generous group of "old grads" available for booster clubs, the typical Ivy League institution prohibits or severely limits fund raising for athletics programs. In addition, the faculty may be all too eager to cut the athletics budget as a way to avoid further curtailment in instructional programs or on the principle of equal sacrifice despite alumni interest or increased student participation. The Ivy League athletes are constantly reminded that they must survive academically in some of the nation's most competitive institutions, despite the long hours that must be devoted to many varsity sports.

The Title IX compliance question exacerbates an already difficult financial problem for the Ivy League. Some Ivy League representatives have argued that there would be no Title IX problem if the rest of the NCAA would simply adopt the Ivy League principle of no financial aid based only on athletic prowess. Ivy League representatives have not been as vocal as some other institutions in their resistance to the more costly HEW draft interpretations of Title IX regulations, but most of their institutions will have to spend substantially more for women's programs than is now the case.

Small Colleges

There are 700 small colleges in the United States. These institutions make up nearly one-fifth of all the nonprofit institutions of higher education; all but about thirty are private institutions. Because these schools are small, the enrollment in these liberal arts colleges accounts for less than 20 percent of total enrollment nationwide. About half of these institutions participate in the NCAA, NAIA, or AIAW, which suggests that such colleges have organized intercollegiate athletics programs.

The typical liberal arts college spends from $100,000 to $150,000 on its athletics program; many institutions spend more. Usually, no grants-in-aid are based entirely on athletic prowess. Athletes are often recruited; any aid to them follows the needs analysis systems applied to other students, with perhaps some "sweetening" added in the form of arranged summer jobs or another self-help component. Any full-time coaches are limited to football and basketball. The athletics program and the physical education program are often closely related: they share facilities and often coaches either have faculty appointments or, more commonly, are faculty members who coach in addition to their other duties, often for little or no additional pay or no released time. Coaches in some sports are part-timers hired exclusively for that purpose. Physical facilities are maintained by the same physical plant department that services the rest of the campus and these costs, along with utilities, are generally absorbed in larger budgets rather than being charged to the athletics program.

Salaries are the largest single item of expenditure of these programs' budgets, followed by travel and equipment. Most such institutions hold down travel costs by participating in local conferences so that there is seldom the need for overnight accommodations and where, except for football, a large van owned by the college can transport all the athletes. As in other kinds of institutions, football in these colleges is the most expensive sport, but it does not dominate athletics the way it does in other institutions for several reasons:

• There are typically no grants-in-aid for any athletes. In contrast, among Division IA institutions, as many as ninety-five football players may be receiving aid.

- There are far fewer assistant coaches in the small colleges and most are part-time employees.
- The major powers often take expensive overnight trips to compete in games in other parts of the nation; even within the major conferences, travel usually involves one or two nights.
- Recruiting costs are much higher in the Division IA institutions than in the small colleges.
- Smaller institutions tend to offer as many varsity sports opportunities as do larger institutions so that football does not dominate the budget as much as it can at the larger institutions.

The budgetary support of intercollegiate athletics in small colleges is generally the same as for any other program of the institution. Students and their families pay for two-thirds of the program's cost through their tuition and, in some cases, through special activity fees. Typically, a college will raise less than $25,000 through ticket sales and, in contrast to the major athletics powers, probably at least half of that income will come from basketball or soccer. Football must generate most of the gate receipt income in the larger institutions, but football attendance is lower in the smaller institutions where there are more basketball games than there are football games. In a few instances, the athletics program can be partially subsidized by renting out facilities or by offering profitable summer camps or operating golf courses for profit. Usually, there are no booster clubs and fund raising is carried on by an all-college development staff. The athletics program is not intended to be even close to self-supporting. Winning or losing makes relatively little difference at the gate. There are clear public relations benefits to success on the field, but there may also be additional costs for travel or recruiting. The fact that the NCAA now uses some of its ABC television contract income to support national championship events in most sports has helped these small institutions, which heretofore had to raise special gifts to send the soccer team to a Division III national championship event.

Small college athletics is participation- rather than spectator-oriented. Athletes are not necessarily among the most admired students on campus and they get no special privileges. The ratio of students participating in intercollegiate athletics to total enrollment is usually much higher than at the larger institutions and there is often relatively little competition to make the team. Despite the low pressure, many sports are physically very demanding, no matter what the setting may be. A good illustration is basketball. A young person must be in good physical condition to play basketball and a typical Division III institution may play the same twenty-five to twenty-seven games that a Division IA institution plays. The season stretches over two semesters or at least longer than one quarter. Not only is the sport demanding physically, but it also requires a major time commitment. There is relatively little glory and no financial aid available (solely for athletic prowess) at the small college so it is often said that many good basketball players do not go out for the team because they do not want to make the time commitment when their first responsibility is to their academic work.

Coaching is much different in a small college than in a large institution. There is less pressure to win and the experience is altogether less ulcer-producing. However, the demands on time can be formidable, the compensation low, and frustrations are many where one is expected to be at least moderately successful without having the resources to produce success. The coach at a large institution is more isolated—although the financial rewards and job risks are higher—than the small college coach. The many part-time coaches at small colleges, who may have full-time jobs elsewhere, may have a rewarding experience of doing what they like in a low-pressure context: their livelihoods do not depend on coaching and they may not have much contact with the institution beyond the student athletes. The full-time faculty member who is the assistant soccer coach may also find the experience pleasurable, if time-consuming, and certainly retains the collegial relationship with his faculty peers.

Small institutions have no financial problems in athletics that are distinguishable from their severe overall financial problem. These institutions are an endangered species, and many may not survive the demographic crunch of the next fifteen years. Relatively few small colleges will likely attempt to survive by eliminating or sharply curtailing their intercollegiate athletics programs because most will realize that such opportunities are important in attracting prospective students. Eliminating athletics might result in high costs and low benefits in terms of potential savings.

The small college faces few problems in complying with the spirit of equal opportunity for women under Title IX. Because football is not the large factor in the budget that it is in larger institutions, and because total budgets are much smaller with little or no financial aid, the absolute gaps in expenditures for men's and women's sports are not large. An AIAW study of NCAA Division III institutions shows they are spending 30 percent of their athletics budgets on women's programs compared with 14 percent for Division I institutions. The participation rates for men and women are not much different (women account for about 30 percent of all participants) in large and small institutions, nor do the number of sports differ much. Typically, a small college could increase its spending on women's programs by $50,000 to $75,000 or less and have achieved dollar parity. The comparable figure for large institutions, with large grants-in-aid budgets and with the budgetary dominance of football, is on the order of several million dollars, although it should be clear that absolute parity of expenditures is not required by Title IX regulations. Indeed, it can be argued that most small colleges have already complied with Title IX if one uses the measure of per capita equality of expenditures in relation to the numbers of male and female participants. The Title IX problems of small colleges may come down to questions of access to facilities, which may be both a scheduling problem (men traditionally get the prime hours for practice) and a physical facilities modification problem (to provide comparable locker and equipment facilities for women). In some cases, it may be necessary to add one or two sports. But generally, it appears that male and female equality in athletics has been attained by many small colleges and can be achieved by most of the others with only modest expenditures.

Mixed Model Institutions

The mixed model comprises about 250 public and private institutions which differ from the semipro model in that they offer fewer athletics scholarships, have significantly lower recruiting budgets, and smaller athletics staffs. Unlike small colleges, these institutions offer some aid based solely on athletic ability and do generate some income and aspire to be nationally competitive in one or two sports.

Currently 178 mixed institutions have chosen active membership in the NCAA and a Division II classification; another eighty institutions belong to NAIA or hold membership in both organizations. This diverse grouping of mixed institutions reflects a comparable diversity of aspirations. Some of the mixed institutions are seeking a big-time status in football and/or basketball. Other mixed institutions are considering avenues for reducing costs of their athletics programs by lowering their classification. For the first group of institutions wanting to elevate their classification, the NCAA has created formidable obstacles, especially in its scheduling requirements. Mixed institutions wanting to "reduce" their classification can eliminate grants-in-aid based only on athletic ability.

Although no official documents are kept by the NAIA on expenditures per institution for grants-in-aid based on athletic prowess, a sampling of these institutions suggests that a majority of the 520 member institutions offer some form of limited athletics grants-in-aid.

Most mixed institutions believe that athletics is important to the life of the institution. At these institutions, athletics plays a visible and vital role within the university community while emphasizing the value of a quality academic program. Chief executive officers of such institutions have consistently stated that collegiate athletics is not only desirable, but also essential to the ongoing student life of that campus. The administrators have also stated that athletics is good for the participating student athletes and provides an opportunity for students and community members to identify more closely with the institution. Such identification is thought to have important value for future institutional support.

Mixed model institutions can be grouped into three major categories: (1) institutions with the financial resources that match their philosophy and aspirations for collegiate athletics; (2) institutions having fewer dollars and resources than needed to achieve the aspirations and goals set forth by the institutions; and (3) institutions that have financial resources in excess of the institution's aspirations for collegiate athletics.

Although all institutions within this study define their athletics programs as auxiliary enterprises, few are self-supporting. An athletics budget for a mixed institution may range between $140,000 and $700,000. Because of the various approaches to budgeting athletics accounts at different institutions, actual expenses incurred by an athletics program vary. For example, some institutions charge maintenance, heating, and lighting of athletics facilities and use of office space to the athletics program, while other institutions charge all such items to a general maintenance and physical plant account. Such approaches to university budgeting are determined by university systems, as well as the individual institution.

Regardless of the budgetary procedures used at the mixed institutions, expenditures for the total athletics program are clearly lower than those at a semipro university. Some major reasons for this difference are: (1) fewer grants-in-aid are offered at mixed institutions; (2) fewer coaching personnel are full-time at these institutions; (3) recruiting costs are lower in the mixed model; and (4) travel expenses are much lower at mixed institutions since traveling squads are smaller and the competition is regional, rather than national. Also, many mixed institutions bill a portion of coaches' salaries to the instructional budget, whereas the full-time coaches at semipro institutions are budgeted as an athletics expense.

Mixed institutions' expenditures for football are about 10 percent of the total expenditures under the semipro model. The expenditure for basketball at mixed colleges is about 20 percent of a semipro basketball program.

Funding for collegiate athletics on public campuses is derived from such sources as activity fees, gate receipts, private contributions, and some general purpose revenue. Whereas most state institutions do not use tax monies for coaches' salaries, athletics supplies, and equipment, private institutions use tuition monies and general fees from the total university budget as a means of supporting athletics. Coaches who have teaching responsibilities have that portion of their salaries drawn from the instructional part of the university budget. Another dimension of concern and long-range planning of collegiate athletics is centered on projections of declining student enrollment, since an important part of many budgets is from student fees. Obviously, a decrease in student enrollment represents decreased monies.

At mixed institutions, the number of sports offered ranges from a minimum of six to a maximum of thirteen for men and from a minimum of one sport to a maximum of ten for women. A majority of the mixed institutions do not have an equal balance of sports for men and women student athletes.

In the mixed institutions, a majority of the athletics programs are separate from departments of health and physical education. Although there are many women's athletics directors on the campuses of mixed institutions, most do not have the same authority or responsibility as the athletics directors for the men's programs. Often, the role of a number of women athletics directors is that of coordinator. Such a coordinator usually reports directly to the men's athletics director regarding scheduling of facilities and budgets. The chairperson for health and physical education programs reports to the chief academic officer while the athletics director often reports directly to the chief executive officer or a senior vice president.

All mixed institutions studied had an athletics committee or council. Many of these committees were advisory and reported directly to the chief executive officer of the institution. The athletics director, although not a voting member, served a major function as an ex-officio member of such committees. The athletics director had the responsibility of preparing and informing the committee of plans, coaching salaries, staff turnovers, scheduling, awards, scholarships, and other such issues.

Due to the ever-restricting budgetary resources, fund raising and promotions have become a more active and essential element of the athletics program. Fund raising was once considered desirable; now it is a crucial aspect of budgeting. The pressures for increased gate receipts and private donations were evident at the institutions in this study. Colleges with the basic characteristics of a mixed model institution have limited opportunities for increased attendance and income. Currently, football and men's basketball are viewed as major revenue-producing activities on most campuses, but attendance data indicate that the overexposure of big-time football on television can negatively affect efforts to increase attendance at mixed institutions. Spectators are becoming more sophisticated and informed due to the ubiquitous communication media. Football at mixed institutions may be perceived as "small time" to such sophisticated audiences and may be removed from the market as other forms of entertainment choices are chosen. Representatives of institutions in the study expressed a guarded optimism that women's basketball would also become a significant revenue producer.

At the mixed institutions, some expenditures could be reduced by cutting existing programs, personnel, or grants-in-aid programs. Some cost cutting could take place by reducing the number of athletics contests now being played and, thus, cutting the cost of travel, lodging, and meals. However, few of these reductions would represent a major percentage of a budget unless football and men's basketball were included. Such reductions would directly affect income productivity. There is little evidence to suggest that athletics directors favor such drastic action. However, some athletics administrators do support reducing or eliminating scholarships in the nonrevenue sports.

Chief executive officers and athletics administrators of mixed institutions who were interviewed expressed a genuine appreciation and understanding of the role intercollegiate athletics plays in an educational enterprise. Therefore, instead of scrutinizing ways to reduce athletics programs, most administrators wished to discover how to maximize financial resources. Mixed institutions are expanding fund-raising and promotional activities to increase dollars at the gate. Booster clubs, which have been virtually nonexistent, are now being evaluated, organized, and implemented as an additional means of generating spectator and financial support.

A basic characteristic of a mixed institution is that it either does not have money to spend on the maximum allotment of grants-in-aid, or it has chosen to be a part of a reduced scholarship program. Therefore, such institutions selectively administer grants-in-aid to programs that have high priority on their campuses. Most such grants-in-aid are provided for the revenue-producing sports.

The mixed institutions have made positive strides in complying with HEW's interpretations of Title IX guidelines and regulations. For a mixed institution to be in compliance budgetarily for women's athletics, 30 percent of a total athletics budget should be apportioned to women's programs. A 1978 AIAW survey indicated that the average total athletics budget in mixed institutions had a 22 percent allocation to the women's programs. Although there has been discussion about the merits of eliminating football and men's basketball programs because of the unequal expenditure they represent, strong feelings and much evidence suggest that such action would financially damage the total athletics program.

The consensus of chief executive officers at the mixed institutions was that collegiate competition has long played an important role in college and university campus life and often has been a major factor in bringing campus and community closer. The administrators also believe that athletics continues to be the phase of education that attracts more community attention than most other areas of school life. At the mixed institution, intercollegiate athletics depends on the support of the community, as well as the university. There was a strong belief that the amount of recognition a successful athletics program receives is invaluable to an institution and it was reemphasized that athletics continues to play a positive role in adding to the total experience of a student's education.

Predominantly Black Institutions

The athletics programs in the more than 100 predominantly black institutions in the United States may be broken down into three categories: (1) programs that do not sponsor football (over a third of the institutions); (2) NCAA Division IAA semipro programs with football (a tenth of the institutions); and (3) small college programs that offer football (over half of the institutions). The financial problems of all these programs are compounded by the precarious financial situations of the institutions themselves in all educational programs and activities. Student enrollments in these colleges range from 2,000 to 4,500. The effect of the current inflation on these traditionally inadequately funded institutions has been horrendous; no relief is apparent in the near future.

Nonfootball programs

About forty predominantly black institutions do not sponsor football programs. Athletics programs in these private, mostly church-supported schools operate with total athletics budgets of $20,000 to $60,000 annually. These institutions are United Negro College Fund schools, which have been forced to drop football programs because of lack of finances and because they receive substantial support from donors who dimly view funneling sorely needed academic funds into sports programs. Men's athletics programs offer two to four sports of which basketball is the only very limited revenue producer. Women's programs offer from one to three sports.

Limited or nonexistent gate receipts dictate general institutional fund support of the athletics program—usually through allocation of 20–30 percent of nontuition student fee income. Facilities are limited; most schools have only one gym or physical education building. Athletics programs are part of the general physical education program. Coaches teach full time and receive minimal release time. These institutions are members of the NAIA or NCAA Division III or both. The financial prognosis for these programs is poor. Current budgets have already been cut back to the bare essentials.

The next cost-cutting step will likely be the dropping of individual sports programs. Unlike athletics staffs at predominantly white institutions and the two other categories of predominantly black institutions, athletics administrators at these nonfootball colleges are not expecting to be saved by alumni donations and general athletics fund raising. These income sources are already severely limited and institutional administrators are not about to try to justify requests for outside support for anything but academic needs. These programs do not have any prospect for increasing gate receipts or student fees. Maintenance of existing skeleton athletics program budgets will be a major accomplishment. Under such circumstances, equalization of opportunities for women may only be achieved by cutting back the limited opportunities currently afforded male students.

NCAA Division IAA

Only eleven predominantly black institutions hold membership in Division IAA of the NCAA. No predominantly black institutions are members of Division IA. However, because there are only thirty-nine institutions in Division IAA football, four or five of these black institutions reap considerable financial benefits from regional television appearances. Average gate receipts, guarantees, and other outside income totaling approximately $200,000 annually are characteristic of athletics programs in this category. Division IA and IAA institutions combined have average total annual budgets of $2.2 million. The average athletics budget of predominantly black Division IAA institutions is about $400,000, which represents a considerable discrepancy. These budgets support six to eight sports for men and four to six sports for women. The areas of greatest expenditures in rank order are: (1) salaries; (2) equipment/travel; and (3) financial aid. In addition to gate receipts, most athletics programs receive 50 percent of the annual general student fee income. Program budgets are based on gate receipts and enrollment estimates from the previous year with monies provided from the institution's general fund in the current year. Therefore, budget reductions resulting from failure to meet projected income levels are usually imposed one year later. These cuts are almost always in the area of travel, equipment, and supplies. Financial aid and recruiting expenditures are seldom reduced because they are perceived to have a direct relationship to income production and maintenance of program competitiveness with other institutions within the division.

These institutions do not have auxiliary enterprises or self-supporting athletics departments. With the exception of head football and basketball coaches, all coaches have other major teaching responsibilities. Men's and women's athletics programs are combined and housed in the physical education administrative unit. Although facilities are not comparable to Division IA institutions, football stadia hold 15,000 to 20,000 spectators and basketball facilities accommodate 5,000 to 8,000 people. Facilities are much better than those at other predominantly black institutions.

Although the athletics programs of these eleven Division IAA institutions are superior to other predominantly black institutions, significant financial problems loom in the near future. Division IAA membership requires that 60 percent of all football games and 85 percent of all basketball games be played against other Division IA or IAA teams. Most of the predominantly black athletics programs have developed in the black athletics conference structures with few Division I opponents other than themselves. They are now forced to break ranks and attempt to schedule predominantly white schools.

Several problems have already emerged because of this scheduling requirement. Historically, NCAA Division I institutions have not been generous in attempting to help the "have-nots" join the "haves." There does not seem to be a racial basis for this reality. Rather, institutions that have a competitive advantage want to keep it. Therefore, scheduling efforts to date have met with mixed success. Grambling State University is able to obtain guarantees to play away from home because of its national reputation. Other black institutions have met significant scheduling resistance which has forced them to travel great distances to play and/or to offer substantial guarantees to attract opposing Division I teams to their home arenas. Both of the latter consequences are financially debilitating to already struggling programs. Many of these institutions are considering raising football and basketball ticket prices to make up these costs. Others are planning to cash in on the influence of former athletes and other alumni who have recently attained corporate executive status by establishing fund-raising programs. Student fee levels are already high and additional general institutional resources are impossible to obtain. These institutions have the ability to make some Title IX compliance progress. They have been primarily using physical education positions to add coaches for women's teams and have been funneling additional student fee income into women's sports.

The prognosis for the financial well-being of Division IAA programs depends on: (1) the successful resolution of scheduling difficulties; (2) no increase in Division IAA membership so as to improve access for predominantly black institutions to television revenues; and (3) success in their efforts to entice alumni to work to support their athletics programs. Unfortunately, these eleven institutions are in the best financial position among all predominantly black institutions but make up only 10 percent of this total population.

Small college programs with football

The majority of the other sixty to seventy predominantly black institutions have athletics programs and sponsor football. These institutions are members of black athletics conferences. The programs support four to six men's and two to five women's sports and have average annual athletics budgets of $150,000 to $200,000. Scholarship budgets are extremely limited but are offset by the eligibility of most black athletes for Basic Educational Opportunity Grants or other aid based on need. Recruiting expenditures range from $5,000 to $8,000 compared with the $10,000 to $20,000 expended in Division IAA programs. However, it is difficult to identify these funds because they appear in budgets as general institutional monies. These programs are classified as NCAA Division II and III and most are also NAIA members. Men's and women's programs are jointly administered under the physical education department; facilities are inadequate.

Inflation has caused severe cutbacks in scheduling, travel, and equipment. Prospects for relief from increased costs are nonexistent. Therefore, many of these institutions will probably be forced to drop sports very soon, football being the first to go. Additional income from fund raising is possible, but student fees and gate receipts are unlikely to increase. Like the United Negro College Fund member institutions, these institutions are under constant pressure to maintain academic programs at the expense of other activities.

In summary, athletics programs at predominantly black institutions are suffering, as are black colleges and universities, from inadequate resources. They have never been adequately supported and the future does not portend any change for the better. Men's athletics programs are in trouble and women's athletics are disastrous. Bare-bones programs will continue to be the rule, rather than the exception.

The Community and Junior Colleges

There are about 1,000 community and junior colleges in America. About 70 percent of these participate in intercollegiate athletics programs. The National Junior College Athletic Association (NJCAA) has 574 members in its men's program and 471 members in its women's program. An additional 104 junior colleges operate in California, plus a few in the state of Washington. Of those institutions participating in intercollegiate athletics, about 90 percent are publicly controlled. The remaining 10 percent are private.

There is no central record-keeping mechanism in the office of the National Junior College Athletic Association for determining the total amount of dollars encumbered for intercollegiate athletics relative to the college budget, but a scattered sample of evidence indicates that the average junior college athletics program spends about 1 percent or less of the institution's total budget.

A typical budget for an athletics program of a junior college may vary from $30,000 to $80,000. Since, in contrast to NCAA rules, there are no restrictions regarding the number of sports an institution is required to offer to be an NJCAA member, some budgets are even smaller; a few are larger. Grants-in-aid based on athletic ability are offered at most institutions in some form. At a number of such institutions, community interest and financial support are crucial to the ongoing success of the athletics program.

Practically all coaches hold joint appointments as instructors within the academic programs, while a number of coaches for the nonrevenue-producing sports are part-time employees. The athletics facilities are maintained under the physical plant maintenance program for the entire campus. These costs, along with those for utilities, are usually absorbed in the total institutional budget.

A typical junior college program will offer between six and eight intercollegiate sports for its men, but some offer as few as four; others have as many as fourteen. For women, the typical offering is between three and five intercollegiate sports; at some institutions as few as two are offered and at others, as many as eight. The budgetary support of intercollegiate athletics in junior colleges is generally the same as for any other department or program of the institution. Football and basketball generate the largest amount of gate income at most institutions, but in some geographic areas, such as St. Louis, soccer is also extremely popular and successful.

A significant problem facing junior college athletics is that the national championship events place an additional financial burden on participating teams. Although some monies are returned to the competing institutions in the sports of basketball and football, total expenses are not covered. Furthermore, the advent of additional women's competition and championship play has complicated the financial problem. One solution is to discover some way to obtain outright sponsorship or guarantees for funding national championship teams.

One way to reduce championship costs in some sports may be to schedule the national championships for some of the men's and women's sports at the same time and at the same site. Such scheduling significantly reduces the cost of tournament personnel. For example, the women's cross country runners compete on the same course as men. Such scheduling procedures for championship play have merit and should be seriously considered for a number of championship events. Currently, the NJCAA receives a $15,000 travel grant from the baseball major leagues to offset baseball expenditures. No other such support has come forth at this time from any other professional sports organization.

During 1974–75, junior colleges were invited to take part in developing an active structure for governing athletics for men and women at the junior college level. In 1975, the NJCAA implemented the total governing organization so that its voting membership was equally distributed between men and women representatives. Governing the junior college's athletics programs, therefore, is determined by both the men and women. This single organization for men and women appears to have been highly successful. Women coaches have had opportunities to be selected for national and international competition that they would not have had otherwise.

Many junior colleges are in small rural towns where the community identifies with the local teams. There is a strong possibility that the current energy shortage might result in additional spectators for junior college sports. Whereas people from these rural towns travel to larger cities to attend college football or other forms of entertainment, they may now stay home for the junior college games.

Alternatives in scheduling nonchampionship games have helped junior colleges reduce athletics travel expenditures. In football, a number of junior colleges are now playing the same institution both at home and away during the same season. Such scheduling of games against close local rivals keeps fan interest high and travel costs low. In basketball, some teams play each other as many as three times in a season, thus maintaining a complete slate of games while cutting travel costs.

NJCAA's attempts to reduce expenditures and unite the men's and women's programs in one structure have yet to generate among junior college presidents major disagreement about its efforts, intentions, and implementation of intercollegiate sports. As the executive director of the NJCAA noted, such support made it possible to integrate the total organization into a men's and women's unit that offers positive athletics opportunities for its members.

Income and Support

The sources of income and support available in intercollegiate athletics are widely varied as might be supposed in light of the great interest these sports can generate among spectators. Despite this variety, some of the principal sources of income are yielding less than they have in the past, while expenditures are going up.

Gate Receipts and Television

For only about 200 institutions in the nation, gate receipts are the largest single source of funds for the intercollegiate athletics program. On the average, gate receipts at these institutions amount to nearly half of the income necessary to support the program. For the members of the College Football Association, gate receipts in general (including concessions) may account for as much as three-fourths of the total budget. These budgets range from $2.5 million to as high as $9 million, although the gate receipts percentage falls off in very high-cost programs.

At those institutions in which gate receipts are a significant source of income, football income usually exceeds basketball income by at least five to one. This ratio is a function principally of the fact that the per game football attendance more than outweighs the larger number of basketball games. Except for universities like Marquette and DePaul, which do not play football and produce net income on basketball, most Division IA institutions earn far more on football than on basketball. Although basketball is seldom more than a break-even sport in the major powers (unless one's institution goes to the "final four" of the NCAA tournament with its rich TV bonanza), football is a big financial winner for Division IA institutions. The typical expectation at a Division IA football institution is that football will generate profits of from $800,000 to $2 million to support the rest of the athletics program. The Raiborn study suggests that only about half of the 139 Division IA institutions with football programs turn a profit on that sport. The number with football deficits appears to be growing each year so that the number of institutions with profitable football programs may actually be as low as fifty or sixty.

These fifty or sixty institutions are under severe constraints in generating more football income. First, competition is keen for the entertainment dollar, particularly in large metropolitan areas, and this elasticity of demand holds down ticket price increases close to the inflation rate. Success at the gate in these areas depends on winning, and the tendency in some of the major conferences is for one or two out of eight to ten institutions to dominate the conference year after year. Institutions in isolated, semirural locations with a tradition of football attendance and relatively few Saturday afternoon entertainment choices are in a better market position, but they are often limited by stadium size. A high proportion of the institutions depending on football profits simply have few vacant seats remaining. For them, price increases may be the only answer to producing more football income. Few of the universities with huge stadium capacities of 80,000 or more spectators fill them regularly. Michigan, Notre Dame, and Ohio State are exceptional. Even very successful teams such as USC and UCLA cannot routinely fill the Los Angeles Memorial Coliseum given other entertainment possibilities in Southern California. A few universities, such as Wisconsin, have high home game attendance (although less than the stadium capacity) despite mostly losing teams.

The national data on football attendance show slow but steady growth through the sixties and then stabilization from 1971 through 1976, followed by a sudden surge in 1978. Total attendance last fall was 34.3 million, contrasted with 20.4 million in 1960. Some of the surge in the past two years is attributable to better attendance at Division II and Division III games. The top seven conferences in football attendance have increased from a per game average of 41,592 in 1970 to 48,215 last fall. During this same period, the national per game average increased only from 10,178 to 10,829. These figures indicate the continued popularity of football as a spectator sport. In light of stadium capacity, the limited number of winners, the ready availability of televised games, and the competition for the entertainment dollar, these figures also indicate real limitations on football gate receipts to finance future cost increases.

Indeed, we believe that one of these factors alone—the overexposure of televised football—has severely limited attendance at live football games.

The Raiborn data suggest that basketball has been growing slightly as a source of income for many institutions. For example, basketball ticket sales nearly doubled for Division IA football institutions between 1973 and 1977 and, yet, because the amounts in question are so much smaller than for football in these same institutions, the overall percentage of total income represented by basketball grew only from 9 percent to 12 percent. In Division IA basketball-only institutions, the overall average basketball income grew from $84,000 to $129,000 in 1977–79. There are about sixty such institutions and they derive two-thirds of their total income from basketball. For most other Division IA institutions, except universities such as the University of California, Los Angeles and those in the Atlantic Coast Conference (where basketball is generally more popular than football), basketball is not the big income producer.

Television and postseason income are largely restricted to men's football and basketball. The biggest money machine in collegiate athletics is the ABC contract with NCAA to broadcast regular season college football. The current contract covering 1978–81 will produce a total of $118 million over the four years or about $30 million annually. The NCAA holds out 8 percent of the funds generated to pay the costs of championship events, which include football and other sports in all three divisions. This provision has been of great help particularly to the small institutions that have had difficulty financing championships in nonrevenue sports. Most of the remaining income goes to the participating institutions; conference rules applicable to most institutions call for equal or nearly equal distribution within the conference. This means, of course, that the haves and have-nots partake equally, which is a source of discontent within some of the conferences that have perennial winners and losers. The lack of a required sharing is a bonanza for strong independents such as Penn State and Notre Dame and leads other perennial conference winners to consider going independent. Football programs benefit from postseason television rights for major bowl games; again the conferences usually require sharing of income after expenses while the independents simply pocket their shares.

There is no analog in basketball of the ABC contract for regular season football games. Many basketball games are televised during the regular season, but most are locally contracted. However, NBC has contracted with NCAA for the Division I basketball championships at the regional and national level in the past few years. Both NBC and NCAA refused to discuss the overall dollar value of this contract but published accounts run as high as $18 million annually. In some cases, there are not the conference-sharing requirements for these games that are applicable to football. Thus, being one of the final four basketball teams can be a financial bonanza to a hard-pressed institution such as DePaul University.

In summary, the Raiborn data support the impression that television income remains a fairly stable share of the income of the major athletics powers—somewhere in the 10 percent range in the aggregate. It is obviously a much larger factor for the major institutions not in conferences and for final four Division I basketball institutions not required to split most of the proceeds with their conferences.

Television, however, poses a dilemma for the intercollegiate sports world. To the extent that potential spectators at minor events prefer to watch a major event on television, those institutions participating in the lesser event—and "lesser" can often simply mean less notoriety rather than a less exciting contest—may be losing out to television. This phenomenon may help to explain why 8 percent of the ABC football proceeds are withheld by the NCAA for supporting championships in which some of the small institutions participate—so to spread the wealth.

It is, of course, not only collegiate football television that competes with collegiate football attendance. Professional football occupies much of the Sunday afternoon and Monday evening prime time. The average football fan may figure that he or she can safely devote one weekend afternoon to watching football and, given a choice, can stay home on Sunday and watch professional football rather than venturing out to the college stadium, fighting for parking, and paying eight dollars for a ticket on Saturday. If a fan really wants to watch two games a week, the Sunday afternoon pro game can be combined with the Monday night pro game or the Saturday afternoon college game.

The success of the college game at the gate is genuinely threatened both by televised professional and college games and by other forms of entertainment. The lack of other such options in communities outside the metropolitan areas and social pressure help keep attendance up at college games at institutions in less populated areas of the country.

Private Giving and Fund Raising

The prevailing attitude at all institutions included in this study is that the most probable source for increasing athletics revenues is private giving. This position is easily explained. Most programs have actively tried to increase gate receipts: stadia were enlarged, ticket prices were raised, and attendance campaigns were initiated throughout the sixties and seventies. However, the gate receipt income data for the last ten years show a decrease in these revenues as a percentage of total income. The reasonable conclusion is that the potential for increasing gate receipt income is extremely limited. The data also indicate a stabilization of student fee income. Athletics programs at mixed institutions, the Ivy League, and small liberal arts colleges have realized significant additional income from institutional funds over the past ten years. However, most athletics personnel agree that this trend cannot continue because the total university budget is reflecting the economic slowdown. Athletics simply cannot continue to take, or be perceived as taking, priority over faculty salary increases and the funding of academic programs. The only major income source for athletics that has not been fully tapped is private giving. All athletics program models seem to be banking on this potential income source.

Semipro athletics programs with Division IA football programs currently receive private gifts ranging from $250,000 to about $1 million annually. The remainder of institutions in this class receive 7–10 percent of their total income from outside contributors. Mixed institutions derive 5–8 percent of their budgets from this source or approximately from $5,000 to $15,000 annually. The larger the budget, the smaller is the percentage of income from contributions. Most Ivy League and small colleges receive less than 2 percent or from $1,500 to $3,000, annually from contributions.

Central to the pursuit of private donations designated for athletics is the offering of perquisites—privileges, material gifts, or recognition in return for donations. The most common structures for granting these "perks" are annual-giving booster clubs, which offer parking, good seats and tickets, special social events, and/or recognition in return for a standard donation. Such clubs were developed with little benefit of fund-raising expertise and are so small that they have not been perceived as detracting from the larger university development effort. Most university representatives interviewed believed that these groups provided a new source of dollars for the university general development program by attracting new friends and reestablishing alumni contacts. This belief was more apparent in institutions where the athletics fund-raising program was closely tied to or under the jurisdiction of the university development office. However, this tie to general institutional development is not common. Most athletics fund-raising programs are external to the university or are administered by the athletics department independently of the university general development program.

The major concern expressed by representatives of most colleges and universities about these external clubs and foundations was that they are able to withhold donations if situations are not what the members think they should be. Representatives of individual institutions did not see themselves as having the power to bring these alumni efforts "inside." Individual institutions and athletics governing organizations should attempt to bring such groups under normal institutional structures so donor control of funds can be decreased and concomitant withholding pressures reduced. Such a policy would also prevent the possible misuse of such funds.

In recent years, semipro programs have had a substantial number of negative experiences with booster groups. In a few cases, these externally housed funds have been used for illegal recruiting and/or for purposes for which they were not designated by the donor. It is not unusual to find major sports coaches, rather than athletics directors, directly in control of such funds. The potential for abuse of such revenues is significantly increased under these circumstances. In addition, a considerable portion of private-giving income may not be reflected in the revenue data because it never reaches institutional accounts. It could reasonably be hypothesized that a portion of recruiting costs for the semipro model may be hidden in this manner.

Only semipro institutions possessed significant endowments. All others were dependent on annual fund raising or one-time gifts to raise comparable money. Most fund-raising programs are geared to enriching annual scholarship funds. That most of these programs are annual does not insure the stability of income sources. Like gate receipts, poor season records can easily undermine budget stability. The tradition of granting perquisites for donations may have a bad consequence in that alumni can come to expect a return for "investing" in athletics programs. Such expectations increase the likelihood of alumni/donor involvement in the administration of programs—a common fear expressed in the majority of interviews.

Several hypotheses may be presented based on present athletics fund-raising practices:

1. The existence of athletics fund-raising groups outside university control is common. These external groups are more likely to exert additional pressures on athletics programs by withholding funds than

are internal fund-raising programs. The likelihood of funds being misused under these arrangements is also greater because funds are not under the direct control of the university.

2. The majority of athletics fund-raising programs are either external to the university or administered by athletics departments separate from larger university development efforts. A continued trend in this direction, coupled with a push for significantly more private gifts, may produce conflicts with nonathletics university development efforts.

3. Athletics fund-raising efforts, in most cases, have not been directed by professional development personnel. Athletics development efforts would be more likely to succeed by the use of such personnel.

4. The tradition of offering perquisites in return for athletics donations can increase donor involvement in athletics program decision making because of the expectation of return.

Neither donor involvement in program decision making nor the expectation of return by donors are characteristics of well-developed fund-raising programs. Reducing these undesirable effects should be a priority of athletics fund-raising programs.

In summary, it seems that significant additional funds over the long term can be obtained through private gifts. However, it is questionable whether such income programs can be expanded at a rate that will keep pace with the rising expenditures of most athletics programs. In addition, athletics programs fund raising may come to conflict with general university development programs.

Other Potential Income

Institutions of higher education are creatively engaged in a variety of programs other than private giving where the cultivation of such efforts might better benefit the institutions by increasing opportunities of raising additional income for the institution, its athletics program, and its staff.

Summer sports camps and clinics, as well as weekend clinics throughout the academic year, are being implemented as a means of producing additional income that may be tapped for hiring staff, upgrading individual athletics programs, maintaining athletics facilities, or supporting nonathletic aspects of the institution. Such camps and clinics offer a real benefit to institutions because they are a visible way of fostering community interest and involvement that may carry over into the regular playing season. Many such camps also offer the opportunity of showcasing the institution to prospective students. The inherent value of camps and clinics should not be taken lightly in today's ever-increasing struggle for student enrollment. Other possibilities for income potential are the rental of athletic facilities for nonuniversity-sponsored events, concerts, various conventions, guest performances, and lectures. For example, at Southwest Missouri State University (Springfield), the rental of the self-sufficient Hammons Center along with promotions, concessions, and parking revenue brought an additional $150,000 to the center.

Additional funds have been forthcoming at a number of private and public institutions where natatorium space, ice rinks, gymnasium facilities, and outdoor recreational courts and fields are rented to outside groups. However, due to the statutes of some states, such rental is not always possible at public institutions.

Many institutions faced with reduced budgets are assigning coaches to academic instead of annual contracts. Coaches, particularly at semipro and mixed institutions, are being given the opportunity to operate camps and clinics during the summer months to earn additional income. Using coaches to run camps and clinics within the university structure during the summer is comparable to the university's hiring instructional staff to teach summer courses. Summer camps and clinics and facilities rental are an increasingly significant element in the development of athletics budgets and shall continue to be important in budget planning.

Costs

The major drains on intercollegiate athletics coffers are those associated with generating income: recruiting, staff, travel, subsidies for student athletes. Exacerbating their effect on already stretched budgets is unyielding inflation. These forces are driving institutions involved in athletics to develop ways of cutting costs without endangering the quality of sports training and competition.

Grants-in-Aid

Most financial aid available to students in colleges and universities to cover tuition, room and board, books, and miscellaneous expenses is awarded on the basis of need. The calculation of need is based on the submission by the student's parents—or by the student if he or she is classified as "independent" according to some rather rigid definitions—of information on income, expenses, assets, liabilities, and family size. That information is processed either by the College Scholarship Service or American College Testing Program or a state agency in the case of state funds. The computer evaluation of the parental information follows national norms to compute the *expected family contribution* for a particular student. The lower the family income and net assets and the larger the family size, the lower will be the expected family contribution. The expected family contribution is then compared with the student expense budget for the institution the student will attend. The basic formula is student expense budget minus expected family contribution equals need.

Need is met in the form of grant, loan, and work, the latter two usually being referred to as "self-help." There are a variety of funding of sources available. The federal Basic Educational Opportunity Grant Program, which has its own needs analysis system through which the funds are awarded directly to the student, is the largest. Other federal programs are the National Direct Student Loan Program, the Supplementary Educational Opportunity Grant Program, and the College Work-Study Program, all three of which are administered through the institution on the basis of an allocation of funds to the institution. Together with the Guaranteed Student Loan Program, these federal programs constitute about two-thirds of the financial aid awarded on the needs basis. State programs are also important, particularly in more populous states with generous programs. Institutional funds usually close any remaining gap or unmet need after allotting federal and state funds.

Most student athletes receiving financial aid have qualified for that aid through the same needs assessment systems as are applied to other students. However, at those institutions with athletics programs in NCAA Division I, and many AIAW institutions, athletes generally receive financial aid without reference to need, solely on the basis of their athletic prowess. Both the NCAA and AIAW limit the number of students so aided and the award per student. Financial aid is so expensive, reaching at least $7,000 per year per student in some expensive private institutions, that relatively few institutions use their full quota of awards and many institutions severely restrict the award per student, providing only partial support, to athletes skilled in sports that do not produce revenue.

Annual grants-in-aid budgets in major institutions can total more than $1 millon, although the average even in NCAA Division 1A institutions is considerably less. The Raiborn study suggests that grants-in-aid may account for 20–30 percent of total expenses in these institutions.

Need-based financial aid has become much more widely available over the past five to seven years, largely as a result of extremely rapid growth in federal need-based programs. At the same time, student expense budgets have risen rapidly as a result of inflation-driven increases in fees charged by institutions. Typically, the NCAA Division I institutions charge the athletics departments for the entire cost of fees charged to athletes. The institutions must generally account for fee income for every registered student; at institutions that award aid to athletes solely on the basis of athletic prowess, the entire cost of that aid (except in some cases for the BEOG award) is a liability of the athletics department even where the student might qualify for federal or other need-based aid.

Institutions interested in cutting costs of athletics programs often suggest subsidizing athletes only on a needs basis to achieve major savings. Several attempts to eliminate subsidies not based on need have failed to pass a number of NCAA annual meetings. To prohibit nonneed aid, national legislation is required; no single institution attempting to compete at the highest levels could hope to recruit top athletes solely on a needs system if competing schools awarded aid on the basis of athletic prowess. Even the neediest students, with negligible expected family contributions, are usually required to have "aid packages," which include loans and work, as well as grants. Subsidized athletes, particularly in football and basketball, usually have "full rides," meaning that all tuition, room and board, and living expenses (subject to the differing rules of NCAA and AIAW) are paid by the athletics program.

The major athletic powers generally oppose moving to a needs-based system because they see a general leveling effect by which they would lose their competitive edge over lesser institutions. Representatives of these schools also argue that the "full ride" system somehow eliminates much of the undercover payment system that was presumably common prior to the present system. Others maintain that using a system that maximizes the use of need-based aid and then supplementing these grants with athletics aid will damage their recruiting ability: the "blue-chip" athlete does not want to be bothered with filling out financial aid forms. Big power representatives also point out that athletes competing at the highest levels of national competition have enormous demands placed on their time. Unlike other students who have time to work, these athletes' practice and competition schedules leave little room for self-help. In addition, they are performing a service to the university, which justifies the "scholarship." Such an argument clearly comes rather close to the cutting edge of the amateur-professional debate. Others maintain that excellence in athletics should be recognized in the same manner as academic excellence. However, academic scholarships are seldom as numerous or as generous as athletics grants-in-aid.

The high cost of grants-in-aid is one of the reasons big-time collegiate athletics have become much more difficult for private institutions to undertake. The tuition gap between public and private institutions ranges from $2,000 to $4,000 per student per year; that difference, plus the sometimes higher academic standards of the more prestigious private institutions, has made it difficult for the Northwesterns, Vanderbilts, and Dukes to compete successfully in football and basketball. (It must be noted that a few private institutions, including Duke and Stanford, have been remarkably successful in recent years.)

The grants-in-aid situation is also a factor in the financial problems created by schools attempting to remedy the disparity between the athletics opportunities available to men and women. Until recently, few, if any, athletics scholarships were available for women.

Title IX of the 1972 Education Amendments may be interpreted as requiring equalization of scholarship opportunities for women in proportion to their participation in athletics. Even though women are only 30 percent of the total athletics population, equalization costs will be so high that institutions will experience a significant budgetary strain, especially private institutions with high tuition costs.

The demands on Division 1A institutions to equalize opportunities will be unique. In football, a larger proportion of male athletes receive athletics grants (as many as ninety-five out of one hundred football players) than in other sports. Although per capita athletics grants are low in the nonrevenue sports, football skews the formula in such a way as to have a significant effect on the provision of equal opportunity. A larger number of women athletes at Division I institutions will be receiving aid than at Division II institutions, where only sixty-five out of one hundred male football players receive aid, thereby reducing the amount of funds required to give Division II women their share.

The lower tuition costs of Division IA institutions and their relative affluence increase the prospects of their being able to afford equalization. In contrast, private institutions may be facing an impossible, or at the very least, an extremely difficult compliance situation.

Since the NCAA removed the prohibition against using BEOG monies in conjunction with athletics grants-in-aid, many athletics programs have achieved a 10–15 percent reduction in their scholarship costs. The scholarship cost savings created by moving to athletics grants covering only tuition and required fees would range from 50 to 70 percent of current budgeted allocations. As the financial crunch continues, it seems likely that the appeal of such a limitation on scholarship expenditures will become greater.

A favorite alternative to the full-scale move to the needs system has been to eliminate full rides in sports other than football and basketball, thereby protecting the revenue-generating sports. These matters will continue to be debated for a long time because grants-in-aid is one area in which there appear to be some possibilities for cost cutting while retaining quality and box-office appeal—so long as all institutions move in tandem.

A discussion of grants-in-aid would not be complete without some mention of summer employment. Semipro institutions often provide lucrative and sometimes undemanding summer jobs to recruits as a way to get the edge on the competition. From interviews during our visits, we conclude that the national rules and enforcement regarding such jobs may be somewhat looser than enforcement of rules on academic year support.

Salaries

Staff salaries and benefits are the largest single expense in most athletics budgets. In those institutions without athletics grants-in-aid, salaries and benefits are usually more than half of the total. For all types of institutions, salaries and grants-in-aid almost always amount to more than half the total expenditures.

The high salaries of a few head football and basketball coaches receive a lot of publicity. Most head coaches, however, receive very modest compensation considering the pressures and the heavy demands on their time. Moreover, there is often a great disparity between the salaries of head coaches and those of assistant coaches. Although head coaches receive most of the publicity, the pressures and the job vulnerability factors apply equally to assistant coaches in the major institutions.

In the semipro programs, coaching and other staff salaries may bear little relationship to other salaries within the institutions unless state laws or personnel regulations require comparability. Typically, the entire staff serves on annual contracts. In mixed state institutions, many coaches and assistant coaches are part-timers; frequently there are joint appointments whereby an assistant coach may also teach in an academic department where part of the salary is charged. In some of these institutions, coaches may receive tenure. Tenure and joint appointments are rare in the major sports of the semipro institutions. In the small colleges, coaches quite frequently teach and often hold tenure and professorial rank. Thus, their jobs are much more secure than at the semipro universities.

It is still quite common for the athletics director to be a man who was a prominent coach. Thus, success in coaching in athletics has historically been the most important qualification for the position of athletics director. Successful coaches—or teachers—do not necessarily make successful administrators and many athletics departments are not well-managed. However, we observed that many athletics departments in major institutions are actually run by a business manager who has often survived several athletics directors.

Coaches in the semipro institutions, as well as some in the mixed institutions, often have the opportunity to supplement their incomes by coaching in clinics and summer camps, giving speeches, appearing on television shows, and undertaking similar activities. For a few well-known head coaches, these opportunities can produce a big income. Most coaches find the profession a rewarding, but not a particularly lucrative way of life.

It has often been suggested that a way to hold down costs in the semipro programs is to reduce the number of assistant coaches, particularly in football. Coaching staffs in football are large, not so much because of the necessities of fielding teams, but because of the demands of recruiting. Assistant coaches devote most of the off-season to recruiting and, increasingly, head coaches are chosen as much for their assumed talents in recruiting as for their win and loss records. Recruiting requires a set of interpersonal skills that may not bear much relationship to one's knowledge of the sport or the ability to coach student athletes. A reduction in coaching staffs is directly related to recruiting. Until some agreements about the "deescalation" of recruiting practices are reached, there will probably not be much progress in reducing the numbers of coaches.

Recruiting costs are almost always understated in an athletics budget because travel is usually the only cost charged to a recruiting budget. The staff time involved is substantial but rarely charged.

Recruiting

The most significant hidden cost in intercollegiate athletics is recruiting. As noted earlier, athletics staff can spend a great deal of time recruiting, which is not charged. Other costs can be obscured because of recruiting rules. Also, such costs for men and women are different, which is a function of recruiting rules. Both men's and women's athletics program staff have developed effective ways of identifying the prospective student athlete. However, some aspects of the process differ, particularly regarding NCAA and AIAW rules limiting off-campus contact with the prospective student.

The NCAA recruiting model allows an institution representative to meet off-campus with an athlete and his family a maximum of three times and to reasonably entertain during these contacts. In addition, institutions may subsidize one visit each by any number of athletes to the college campus. A prospective student athlete may not make any more than six paid visits to six different institutions. AIAW does not permit a coach or institutional representative to meet with an athlete or her family off-campus. Therefore, no off-campus entertainment costs are incurred. Although coaches are subsidized to assess talent (watch contests) under both NCAA and AIAW rules, the number of such trips in the AIAW system is significantly fewer than those undertaken by coaches of men's teams. In addition, AIAW does not permit subsidizing athletes' visits to campus. The cost differences are obvious.

Interviews indicated that significant abuses were apparent in the NCAA system. Prospective athletes seem to be taking advantage of subsidized visits by traveling to institutions farthest away whether or not they are interested in attending those schools. In major sports, one or more assistant coaches may be on the road full-time keeping close contact with prospects. Coaches in the major sports will attend every game of a high school "blue-chip" athlete to assure the prospective student that the college is seriously interested. The AIAW rules also have flaws. One is that athletes who cannot afford to visit institutions cannot be subsidized and, therefore, are at a considerable disadvantage compared with those prospective students who could attend on-campus scholarship auditions. There seems to be little question that recruiting can be more restrictive without damaging an institution's ability to identify and attract the accomplished athlete as long as such restrictions are not unilaterally adopted. National legislation is needed to guarantee fair competition among institutions in the recruiting process.

There are a number of reasons why recruiting costs are hidden. In semipro athletics programs:
1. Many recruiting costs may be financed by external support groups;
2. In many institutional budgets, recruiting costs are not separated from travel as a general athletics budget line item or they may not appear as an operating expense at all because funds from separate or internal accounts are used;
3. There is no record of the time spent by athletics department employees on recruiting although every indication is that such time is extensive;
4. Telephone budgets are not broken down to reflect recruiting versus administrative expenses, even though telephone recruiting costs are estimated by most Division IA athletics directors interviewed as being in excess of $50,000 annually; and
5. Publicity budgets are not broken down to reflect postage costs or the production of recruiting brochures and other materials although athletics directors indicate that such brochure production is primarily geared toward recruiting and can cost more than $25,000–$30,000

annually. In other athletics program models, these same factors operate but the cost is significantly less. In addition, the smaller programs commonly use regular admissions office personnel in recruiting prospective student athletes.

It is not unreasonable to estimate that the average cost of recruiting in a semipro athletics program is over $400,000 annually when both personnel and other expenditures are considered. At mixed institutions, average costs may range from $10,000 to $30,000 annually; other athletics program models may be expending between $3,000 and $6,000 per year on the average. These estimates are far from insignificant when compared to total program costs. Recruiting expenditures are extremely difficult to measure but they cannot be ignored.

Another factor in recruiting costs to consider is the "beat the Jones" syndrome. If one institution starts a new recruiting practice or offers a new benefit to attract the student athlete, all the others, like dominoes, follow. Other institutions competing for the same student athlete have to adopt the practice to maintain recruiting competitiveness. Training tables, single rooms for athletes, athletics dormitories, carpeted rooms for athletes, etc., are good examples of benefits that require significant capital expenditures. Yet, the positive effect of such practices on winning and losing contests has never been demonstrated. It seems reasonable to assume that strict control in these areas could result in substantial savings.

The potential for reducing costs is great without damaging the effectiveness of the recruiting effort or jeopardizing the existence of fair competition between institutions for student athletes. However, national athletics governing bodies will not have an easy task in determining what activities are essential to the process and which may be eliminated without affecting their programs. The way to finding a middle ground may lie somewhere between the existing NCAA and AIAW systems. The more important question is whether these governing associations will tackle the issue and attempt to control recruiting costs.

Transportation

A continuing financial concern of people involved in intercollegiate athletics is the spiraling cost of transportation. Gasoline prices alone have increased more than 60 percent since January 1979. Significant additional women's programs have developed in the past few years, which have increased costs. Growing athletics programs represent a need for increased travel at higher costs. Institutions that once had chartered flights now take commercial flights sparingly or travel extensively by bus. For nonrevenue-producing sports, squads often travel by van and automobile, which adds a high liability risk factor to an institution's insurance.

Squad size has been reduced to save money for additional meals and lodging. Efforts have been made to piggyback scheduling in order to use one bus for two or more institutions or more than one team within the same institution. For example, during the 1978 soccer season, the University of Wisconsin-Green Bay and the University of Wisconsin-Parkside shared the expenses for a bus to O'Hare Airport in Chicago, Illinois. Both schools saved money by qualifying for the group discount rate, which would have been unattainable for just one institution. Some institutions are now scheduling two separate sporting events at the same site in order to transport two squads and still save money on transportation. Modest scheduling innovations have been accomplished at some institutions, but indications so far are that little has been done at most other institutions to reduce transportation costs.

In light of the energy crisis, transportation becomes a major factor for all athletics programs. If constructive means cannot be achieved in scheduling athletics events to shorten distances to travel for games and to combine travel by squads, then it may be necessary to consider limiting athletics contests. Reducing the number of athletics events could well be counterproductive because gate receipts would be decreased. Such action would further jeopardize the nonrevenue-producing sports because they are the least financially secure in most athletics departments.

Women's Athletics

The significance of women's athletics programs in the governing and financing of collegiate athletics is as substantial as the question of how to stem the tide of excess expenditures over revenues in men's athletics programs. In 1972, Congress passed the Higher Education Amendments, Title IX of which prohibited sex discrimination in the provision of equal opportunity in educational programs and activities. Title IX provides that, "No person in the United States shall on the basis of sex, be excluded from participation in, be denied the benefits of, or be subjected to discrimination under any educational program or activity receiving federal financial assistance."[7] The regulations for the law went into effect on July 21, 1975. Institutions were directed to conduct a Title IX self-evaluation by July 21, 1976, and were given three years to bring their programs into compliance. Few institutions were in full compliance with the requirements of the statute with regard to their intercollegiate athletics programs by the July 21, 1978 deadline.

In December 1979, the U.S. Department of Health, Education, and Welfare issued a final policy interpretation to clarify any ambiguities in the 1975 regulations.[8] Compliance reviews and more than 100 complaint investigations are scheduled for 1980. Intercollegiate athletics for women have been rapidly growing since the passage of Title IX. Nationwide, women's athletics programs are one-half to two-thirds of the way toward being in compliance. In addition, there seems to be no indication that men's athletics programs have suffered a loss of monies redirected toward funding women's athletics. In fact, men's athletics expenditures since 1973–74 have increased by more dollars than the increase in total dollars allotted to women's athletic programs during this same period.[9] Despite this data, the prevalent myth is that women's athletics and Title IX will mean the death of big-time men's athletics.

The underlying causes of the resistance of many institutions to Title IX in the area of athletics is a lack of understanding of the requirements of the law and a fear of being unable to maintain the men's athletics programs while increasing the financial support of women's programs. Many institutions feel that Title IX will force them to spend as much money on their women's athletics programs as they do on their existing men's programs. A careful reading of the regulations and draft interpretations being considered by HEW indicates:

1. Dollar-for-dollar parity in expenditures is not required.
2. Legitimate differences in the nature of a sport, the level of competition, and other nonsex-related expenditures are not factors in equating men's and women's athletics. Examples of "deductibles" are the high

7. U.S. Department of Health, Education, and Welfare, "Nondiscrimination on the Basis of Sex," *The Federal Register*, vol. 40, no. 108, 4 June 1975, pp. 24128–24145.
8. U.S. Department of Health, Education, and Welfare, "Title IX and Intercollegiate Athletics: Nondiscrimination on the Basis of Sex in Education Programs and Activities Receiving or Benefiting from Federal Financial Assistance," *The Federal Register*, vol. 43, no. 238, 5 December 1979, pp. 58070–58076.
9. Raiborn, *Revenues and Expenses of Intercollegiate Athletic Programs*, p. 22.

cost of conducting major spectator events such as ticket office, concession, and event management expenses.

3. Immediate provision of equal opportunity (not equal aggregate expenditures) for female athletes is required.

4. Equal per capita expenditures proportionate to participation levels are required in the area of financial aid based on athletic ability.

Taking permissible nonsex-related expenditures into account, equal opportunity for female athletes based on current participation levels should cost from 20 to 25 percent of the current athletics budget.

Title IX also addresses expansion of women's programs to meet the needs and abilities of female athletes. No time frame is designated and the method of assessing these needs and abilities is left to the discretion of the institution. Therefore, it is feasible to assume that women's athletics participation may at some time increase from 30 to 50 percent of the total athletics population since most student populations are 50 percent male and 50 percent female. The financial implications of this program expansion are obvious. Assuming most institutions are 50–75 percent of the way toward full compliance based on current participation levels (semipro institutions are on the low side and other models are farther along), women's athletics program budgets may reasonably be expected to double over the next five to ten years.

Because the standard of equal opportunity in athletics must be calculated in relation to the opportunity level that already exists in the men's athletics program, it is logical to assume that women's athletics cannot be immune from the excess expenditures spiral affecting men's athletics programs. Another important factor in the future of women's athletics programs is that they have had neither the time nor the investment to become revenue producing. Therefore, expenditures on women's programs can be offset by only minimal additional income. On one hand, the law requires an opportunity standard based on existing men's practices. On the other hand, this opportunity cannot be afforded by using the existing men's practice of requiring revenue production to offset expenditures. (This revenue-producing expectation is more apparent in semipro institutions which are dominated by self-supporting financial policies.)

Although every institution visited had significantly increased athletics opportunities and funding for their women's athletics programs, this equal opportunity progress was funded by *both* the men's and other general institutional resources. Most institutions have obviously attempted to supplement athletics resources with university general funds to comply with Title IX in order to maintain the quality of their men's athletics programs. Raiborn's data indicate that mixed institutions fund 60–70 percent of their women's athletics programs from institutional resources. Small liberal arts colleges and the Ivy League derive 85–95 percent of women's athletics funds from other than men's athletics sources, while semipro institutions utilize 35–40 percent of institutional monies to support women's programs. The men's athletics program in a semipro university is more likely to be expected to assume a large part of the financial responsibility for women's athletics than the men's program at other kinds of institutions.[10]

AIAW data indicate that women's athletics expenditures are considerably lower than those for men's athletics.[11] Women's budgets range from 14 to 30 percent of the total athletics budget with more progress being evident in mixed, Ivy League, and small liberal arts institutions where equal opportunity costs less in total dollars. Semipro programs have not made as much progress in terms of percentage of total budget, although their dollar outlays have been considerable. For instance, NCAA Division I institutions spent, on the average, $27,000 on their women's programs in 1973 (2 percent of the total athletics budget). In 1978, that figure had grown to $276,000—or 14 percent of the total athletics budget—which is one-half to two-thirds of the way toward Title IX compliance. Several institutions in the country support women's athletics budgets at or near the million dollar mark.

The administration of women's athletics programs is extremely varied. A trend toward merged athletics programs seems to be developing for several financial reasons: (1) to keep down the number of higher level administrative positions; (2) to avoid major equipment duplication; (3) to use space, utilities, etc., more efficiently. However, the cost to women in administrative and coaching positions under merged administrative structures has been considerable. The number of male coaches in women's athletics had increased by 159 percent in the last five years.[12] In almost all instances, when departments have merged, the top job has gone to the men's athletics director. Although the dollar cost of Title IX compliance to men's athletics may be considerable, it is becoming apparent that the human cost to women is also significant.

10. *Ibid.*, p. 46.
11. The Association, *Competitive Division Structure Implementation Survey*, p. 11.
12. Bonnie L. Parkhouse and Milton G. Holmen, "Multivariate Considerations in the Selection of Coaches for Female Athletes: Trends and Issues," (MS, August 1979).

A consequence of the sub-merger of women and women's athletics within the larger construct of men's athletics may be the loss of an opportunity to explore other directions in the development of athletics programs. The real cost of such a loss is incalculable. For instance, it is difficult to explore the effect of different recruiting methods within the existing men's athletics model. Resistance to change in these methods is inevitable because the men's programs fear that any loss of recruiting effectiveness would damage prospects of winning and, therefore, affect their financial well-being. Women's athletics has been able to adopt a recruiting method that costs less than 5 percent of current men's expenditures in semipro institutions while retaining similar effectiveness in attracting talented athletes. It seems reasonable to believe that an independent course for women's athletics might well result in a significant, long-term contribution to exploring cost-control methods without risking loss of the revenue-producing ability of existing men's programs. The potential of the experimental arena provided by independent women's athletics programming should not be ignored. Pushing women's athletics into the same mold as men's athletics may compound the problem of the financial future of intercollegiate athletics. At institutions awarding athletics scholarships, the cost of providing such opportunities to women athletes was without exception a primary concern. The private semipro institutions were the hardest hit on this count because their tuition costs are so high.

A surprise from the visits to the various institutions was that many athletics directors mistakenly believed that Title IX requires *equal expenditures* on men's and women's athletics. As noted earlier, especially at semipro institutions, significant event management expenses do not come under calculations of equal opportunity costs. Clearly, administrators need to have a clear understanding of equal opportunity requirements as they relate to expectations of equivalent expenditures. Myth, rather than fact, appears to be guiding institutional interpretation of Title IX compliance requirements. The consequence of uninformed interpretation of the regulations is that it inhibits the joint resolution of the compliance problem and promotes the continued existence of unrealistic fears about the actual cost of compliance.

The financial future of women's athletics program development is as follows:

1. Expenditures on women's athletics programs will double by 1981 based on the assumptions that (a) institutions are about two-thirds of

the way toward providing equal opportunity; and (b) the effect of inflation over the last several years will continue over the next several years.

2. Women's athletics expenditures will not be offset by even minimum revenues by 1981. Women's athletics programs (a) are not currently producing substantial revenues; (b) do not include a major revenue-producing sport such as football; and (c) need at least a decade (in the opinion of most women athletics directors) to make basketball, volleyball, and/or gymnastics programs self-supporting or significantly revenue producing.

3. Women's athletics program expansion will require a substantial investment by 1981 if existing opportunities for male athletes and general student population proportions remain constant. Several facts support this contention: (a) approximately equal numbers of male and female students make up current enrollments in most institutions; (b) female athletes currently are 30 percent of all athletics participants; and (c) Title IX requires that the interests and abilities of female athletes be met to the same extent as those of male athletes.

4. Over half to 95 percent of the monies spent on women's athletics will come from institutional rather than athletics resources if the current funding sources of women's athletics programs do not change and/or the current deficit status of men's athletics programs does not improve.

5. It is highly unlikely that institutions will be able to afford women's athletics programs without adopting more reasonable cost-control measures in men's athletics in order to slow or eliminate the growing deficit spiral in these programs. The deficit problem is of greater magnitude than that of funding women's athletics.

Men's athletics programs have adopted more cost-control measures since the passage of Title IX than in any other previous period in history of men's athletics. Equal opportunity for female athletes might very well turn out to be the long-needed catalyst for controlling the cost of intercollegiate athletics.

Conclusions and Recommendations

The purpose of this study was to draw some conclusions about the financial condition of intercollegiate athletics programs. It reflects the interest of the Commission on Collegiate Athletics of the American Council on Education in learning more about the topic. With the exception of the Raiborn study, which has been cited, very little is known about the financial health of the athletics enterprise.

In undertaking this study, we concluded for reasons set forth subsequently that it would not be feasible to conduct the study by written means. The state of the art does not permit that and we settled upon the approach of visiting a representative sample of the colleges and universities in the nation. The observations from these visits with athletics directors and chief executive officers, together with further conversations, reading, and our own knowledge of the field, are our data base.

We have organized the body of the report by relevant institutional type and by categories of income and expense. Our findings can be summarized as follows:

1. A financial categorization scheme in intercollegiate athletics would distinguish between those relatively few institutions with highly visible and intensive programs which are operated as largely self-supporting auxiliary enterprises, and those much less visible but more numerous programs which are supported largely through the general budget of the institution in a manner similar to their academic programs. The major characteristic of the former group is their dependence on gate receipts from football to support a costly, multisport athletics program.

2. Contrary to the conventional wisdom, our belief is that a maximum of about sixty institutions in the nation operate football programs which more than break even. Included within the sixty are most of

the major athletics powers of the nation and about 10 percent of the enrollment in colleges and universities. These sixty institutions realize football profits of up to $2 million, but generally less than $1 million. A strict cost accounting for athletics department overhead, maintenance, and other costs not generally distributed by sports would probably reveal smaller profits from football.

3. Except for a few universities, mostly those not in conferences that require sharing of television and bowl game income, supposedly self-supporting athletics programs are not budgetarily profitable. Inflation has exceeded the increase in traditional income sources, particularly gate receipts.

4. Title IX of the 1972 Education Amendments forbids sex discrimination in the programs of any institution receiving federal funds. The legislation, even without significant enforcement action to date on the part of the U.S. Department of Health, Education, and Welfare, has resulted in major increases in the commitment of resources to athletics programs for women. Institutions with men's programs budgets ranging from $2 to $3 million or more are spending from $300,000 to $500,000 and up for women's programs today, when four and five years ago they were spending less than $50,000. Thus, the growth rate of women's programs has generally been considerably more rapid than that of men's programs, but the absolute dollar increase in men's programs has been greater than that of women's programs.

5. Football occupies a peculiar paradoxical position in relation to women's athletics. In the sixty or so institutions with financially profitable football programs, football is the money machine that supports all other sports for men and women. The existence of all other sports depends directly on the ability of the football program to generate the funds to support them. Football, however, is a uniquely expensive sport and is the primary reason why, despite the large increases in women's programs in recent years, a large gap persists between the amount spent on men's and women's sports, computed either in absolute terms or per participant. The curtailment or deemphasis of football, whatever its merits otherwise, would be clearly both politically and budgetarily foolish and not in the interest of other men's and women's programs, which depend on it for their existence.

6. Given uncontrollable and legally mandated expenditures that have outstripped gate receipt increases, many institutions have turned to private fund raising and a few institutions are now approaching $1

million in gifts earmarked for athletics. These funds usually come through booster clubs sponsored and controlled by the athletics department, but in a few instances, they are raised and controlled by separately incorporated foundations or clubs that may then come to have a disproportionate impact on policy decisions, including the tenure of coaches. Representatives of most institutions we visited believe that the potential of athletics fund raising greatly exceeds the considerable efforts that many institutions have devoted to it—many view it as the most promising source of future funds. We detected that a few institutions are hesitant to move vigorously on this front either because of the competition for the funding of higher priority fields within the institution or the fear that more restricted funds will bring more external influence to bear on a program which already has a lot of such influences.

7. Big-time intercollegiate athletics is increasingly limited to the public universities. The extremely high tuitions and high admissions requirements of the major private universities have created a situation in which only 20 percent (thirteen of sixty-two institutions) of the membership of the College Football Association and 24 percent of the membership of the NCAA Division IA (with football) are private institutions (thirty-four of 139 institutions). Suggestions that private institutions simply waive tuition for athletes are shortsighted: the result would be that the waiver would be paid from other than athletics funds or that the institution would increase its enrollment by an amount sufficient to produce the tuition income lost to free-tuition athletes.

The financial problems of most intercollegiate athletics programs are part of the general financial problem of the institutions. Stable or declining enrollments and the ravages of inflation have endangered many institutions and forced some degree of austerity on most. We have no particular advice for these kinds of institutions except that the opportunity to participate in intercollegiate athletics is important for many students and caution should be exercised in applying budget cuts of greater severity to athletics than to some other activities of the institution.

For those institutions where the athletics program fits the semiprofessional or mixed models, we have a few observations. First, we have noted that most of these institutions have seen the salvation of their programs as being the raising of additional income rather than curbing costs. The additional income for most of these institutions is thought to come increasingly from gifts; for some, it is assumed that gate receipts can pay for an increasing share of total costs. We advise caution on both counts. Private fund raising will invariably compete with the general university efforts and will inevitably give more influence in personnel decisions and program emphasis to the donor groups.

We think the evidence is clear that television has already and will eventually depress the live audience market and, thus, gate receipts. Notwithstanding NCAA's "share-the-wealth" program for football on television, the rich will get richer both in television income and gate receipts. Institutions with less successful teams and those outside the College Football Association will find themselves increasingly impoverished by their inability to sell their product.

We think the NCAA should do more to protect the live audience by more careful rationing of the televised product. We would prefer selling much less television for a little less money to the present practice of selling much more television for much more money, at the expense of live events.

In our view, the answer to rising costs in athletics, particularly in football, lies in multilateral cost cutting carefully orchestrated so as not to affect the quality of competition or jeopardize further the nonrevenue-producing sports. Such action must be rigidly enforced by the national governing associations. Cost cutting should focus on grants-in-aid, which we believe should be placed on a needs basis, and on recruiting costs. By reducing the latter, coaching staffs can be reduced, particularly in football. The orchestration of such disarmament will have to proceed under academic presidential leadership outside the framework of the national governing associations. We would urge a carefully phased "SALT" process; the initial negotiations would be carried on through small groups of college presidents and athletics directors and subsequently ratified by the national governing associations.

The authors of this report differ on the subject of national governing structures. Atwell and Grimes argue that the present division of NCAA and AIAW complicates athletics. Although rule differences do not necessarily indicate unequal treatment, inconsistent rules often result in confused program administration at the campus level. Lopiano believes that most talk about merged structures is tantamount to the NCAA submerging the AIAW, which would be an unacceptable outcome to all three authors. Lopiano further believes that the AIAW, which has been in existence only since 1972, should have an opportunity to provide separate leadership and nurturing for women's programs and for testing some alternative and possibly cost-effective approaches to such undertakings as recruiting. A plurality of governing organizations most certainly makes administration more complex. However, several governing bodies as opposed to one offer the advantage of testing various athletics model and may prevent the self-perpetuating, change-resistant characteristics of single monolithic bureaucracies. Atwell and Grimes believe that an alternative governance structure must be designed for all of collegiate athletics, at least in the four-year institutions. The new organization would not necessarily resemble the present structures of the NCAA or the AIAW. We would hope that the "SALT" negotiations we are suggesting could address the question of structuring such an organization. We would see it as being presidentially dominated with the continued participation of athletics directors and faculty members and with considerable student participation.

In our view, a new governing structure would need to have equal participation of men and women, at least until more progress has been made in equalizing the participatory opportunities for men and women. A disturbing development in recent years is that while athletics opportunities for women have increased substantially, the trend toward merged athletics departments has almost always resulted in the director of women's athletics being subservient to the male director and reduced numbers of female coaches. We know of no instance in a major institution where a merged department has been followed by the appointment of a woman as director of athletics. We would not want the kind of merger that results in unequal leadership at the national governing level.

The recent actions of the NCAA and NAIA to initiate women's championships will affect the "SALT" negotiations. Men and women agree that a single national governing body, carefully planned and conceived and using the best provisions of all existing governing bodies, is most desirable. Such unification can only come about from extensive discussion, hard-fought compromises among equals negotiating from positions of strength and strong philosophical commitment. Any effort by men's athletics governing bodies to "take over" women's athletics (despite the objection of women in athletics) exacerbates an already tenuous relationship between organizations and promotes an atmosphere of suspicion and distrust. Negotiations for the common good cannot take place in such an atmosphere. 6037162

The authors strongly urge immediate presidential attention to the problems caused by the initiation of women's championships by the NCAA and NAIA. Ms. Lopiano would urge a moratorium on the initiation of championship events by the NCAA and NAIA and all three authors would urge presidents to inform themselves and enter the debate.

DATE DUE